Mind Over Gray Matter

A Voyage Through Neuropsychology

Freudian Trips

Copyright Page

Disclaimer

The views and opinions expressed in this book are those of the author(s) and do not necessarily reflect the official policy or position of any other agency, organization, employer, or company. The contents of this book are for informational and educational purposes only and are not intended to serve as professional advice, diagnosis, or treatment.

The information provided in this book is believed to be accurate and reliable as of the date of publication. However, it may include some errors or inaccuracies, and no warranty or guarantee is provided regarding the accuracy, timeliness, or applicability of the content.

Readers are encouraged to consult with professional philosophers, educators, or other qualified professionals where appropriate for personalized advice. The author(s) and publisher shall not be liable for any loss, damage, or harm caused or alleged to be caused, directly or indirectly, by the information or ideas contained, suggested, or referenced in this book.

By reading this book, the reader acknowledges and agrees that they are solely responsible for how they interpret and apply the information contained herein.

This book may also include references to other works, studies, and sources. These references are provided for further reading and exploration and do not imply endorsement or validation of the specific theories, viewpoints, or interpretations presented in those works.

Prologue: The Brain's Symphony

Welcome to the wondrous world of neuropsychology, where every thought, memory, and emotion plays out like a symphony in the brain. This is a journey not just through the intricacies of the mind but also through the pages of history, unraveling how our understanding of the brain shapes our comprehension of human behavior.

A Journey Through Time

Our story begins centuries ago, with curious minds wondering about the magic behind our thoughts and actions. Early philosophers pondered whether the heart or the brain was the seat of the soul. The journey through time shows us how ideas evolved, from the brain being a mere cooling system for the blood to being recognized as the command center of our being.

The Brain: A Masterful Conductor

Imagine an orchestra, each musician playing a vital part in creating a harmonious melody. Now picture the brain as a masterful conductor, orchestrating a complex network of cells, known as neurons, to produce every thought, feeling, and movement. Each neuron is like a musician in this grand orchestra, communicating with one another through electrical and chemical signals, creating the symphony of our consciousness.

Neuropsychology: Decoding the Symphony

Neuropsychology is like having a front-row seat to this symphony, providing us with tools to understand how different sections of the brain work together to create the music of our minds. It helps us grasp how we learn new things, why we remember certain events but forget others, and what happens in our brains when we experience emotions.

Relevance in Our Lives

But why does this matter to us? Neuropsychology is not just for scientists and doctors. It touches every aspect of our lives. It helps educators develop better teaching methods, informs therapists on how to treat mental health issues, and guides everyday decisions about our health and wellbeing.

A Preview of What's to Come

In the chapters ahead, we will explore the brain's amazing capabilities, the challenges it faces when things go wrong, and the incredible potential for healing and adaptation. From the basic building blocks of the brain to the complex phenomena of memory and consciousness, we will unravel the mysteries of the mind in a way that is accessible and engaging for all.

As we embark on this journey, remember that understanding the brain is not just about scientific knowledge. It's about understanding ourselves, the people around us, and the intricate symphony that plays within each of us, every moment of our lives.

Welcome to the symphony of the brain. Let the music begin.

Chapter 1: The Neurons' Dance

Imagine a grand ballroom filled with dancers, each moving in perfect harmony with one another. This image beautifully mirrors the world of neurons – the tiny, yet mighty cells in our brain. In this chapter, we embark on an engaging journey to discover the dance of neurons, the basic units of our brain, and how they shape our thoughts, feelings, and actions.

What is a Neuron?

A neuron is like a specialized dancer in the brain's ballroom. Each neuron has a unique structure, consisting of three main parts: the cell body, dendrites, and axon. Think of the cell body as the dancer's core, where all the energy and control resides. The dendrites are like outstretched arms, ready to receive signals from other neurons. The axon is akin to a long, trailing ribbon that carries messages away to other neurons.

The Dance of Communication

Neurons communicate in a fascinating way. When a neuron receives a signal, it generates an electrical pulse that travels down its axon. This electrical pulse is like a dance move, signaling other neurons to respond. At the end of the axon, the electrical pulse triggers the release of chemicals called neurotransmitters, which are like the music that guides the dance. These neurotransmitters cross tiny gaps called synapses to reach neighboring neurons, continuing the intricate dance of communication.

Neural Networks: The Ballroom of the Brain

Our brains contain billions of neurons, all connected in a vast network. Like dancers holding hands in a grand ballroom, these neurons form intricate patterns and pathways. These networks are responsible for everything we do – from simple tasks like blinking to complex ones like solving a math problem or falling in love.

The Dynamics of Neurotransmitters

Neurotransmitters are the essence of the neurons' dance. They are the messengers that influence our mood, thoughts, and behaviors. Some neurotransmitters, like serotonin and dopamine, are like the rhythm of upbeat music that lifts our mood and keeps us motivated. Others, like GABA, are like a slow, calming melody that helps us relax and sleep.

Why This Dance Matters

Understanding the dance of neurons and neurotransmitters is crucial. It helps us comprehend how learning and memory work, why certain drugs affect our mood and behavior, and what goes wrong in neurological disorders like Alzheimer's or depression.

In Conclusion

As we close this chapter, imagine the neurons in your brain, dancing gracefully, communicating through their electrical and chemical signals. This dance is happening in your brain right now as you read these words, shaping your thoughts, emotions, and every aspect of your being. The dance of neurons is not just a scientific concept; it's the very essence of our existence, the rhythm of our life.

Stay tuned as we delve deeper into this incredible world, where each discovery about our brain leads to a greater understanding of ourselves.

Chapter 2: Wiring the Mind's Circuitry

Welcome to a fascinating journey through the mind's intricate circuitry. Just like a bustling city with different neighborhoods, each with its unique role, the brain is made up of various regions that work together to create the magic of thought, emotion, and action. This chapter will take you through these regions in a simple and engaging way, helping you understand the marvel that is your brain.

The Grand Map of the Brain

Imagine the brain as a detailed map, with each area marked for a specific function. These areas are like different departments in a large company, each responsible for a particular type of task, yet constantly communicating with each other to keep the business running smoothly.

The Front Desk: The Frontal Lobe - At the front of the brain is the frontal lobe, much like the reception area of a company. This lobe is in charge of complex thinking, decision-making, planning, and even personality. It's where we process ideas, make plans for the weekend, and decide right from wrong.

The Creative Department: The Parietal Lobe - Located near the top and back of the brain, the parietal lobe is like the creative department. It helps us understand and interact with the world around us, managing our senses of touch and spatial awareness. It's the part of the brain that helps you catch a ball or navigate a new city.

The Media Center: The Occipital Lobe - At the back of the brain is the occipital lobe, the brain's own media center. This area is all about vision, processing everything we see from colors and shapes to motion.

The Sound Studio: The Temporal Lobe - Situated on the sides of the brain, the temporal lobes are like sound studios. They're crucial for processing sounds and language, and they play a key role in storing memories.

The Communication Network: Neural Pathways

The brain's regions communicate through pathways, much like phone lines connecting different departments of a company. These pathways carry messages in the form of electrical impulses, allowing the brain's regions to work together seamlessly. When you speak, for example, your frontal lobe works with your temporal lobe to choose the words and your motor cortex to move your mouth.

The Control Room: The Brainstem and Cerebellum

Beneath these lobes lies the brainstem, akin to a control room. It takes care of the things you don't think about but are vital, like breathing, heart rate, and sleeping. Attached to the brainstem is the cerebellum, the brain's coordinator of movement and balance, helping you walk, dance, or ride a bike smoothly.

Why This Matters

Understanding the brain's anatomy is like having a map to human behavior and cognition. It helps us appreciate how incredibly well-designed our brain is, and it's the first step towards understanding how things can go wrong in neurological disorders.

In Conclusion

As we wrap up our tour of the brain, remember that each part of this magnificent organ is working tirelessly to help you experience the world, form memories, and express yourself. It's a harmonious and complex system that defines who we are and how we navigate our lives. The brain is not just an organ; it's the conductor of the symphony of our existence.

Chapter 3: The Plastic Orchestra

Imagine an orchestra where the musicians can seamlessly switch instruments and adapt to new melodies. This flexibility is akin to a remarkable feature of our brain known as neuroplasticity. In this chapter, we'll explore how our brain adapts, learns, and heals, making it a plastic orchestra capable of extraordinary transformations.

Neuroplasticity: The Brain's Flexibility

The brain's capacity to rearrange itself by creating new neural connections throughout life is known as neuroplasticity. This ability is like a musician learning to play a new instrument or adapting to a new tune. It means our brains are not rigidly mapped out but are dynamic and adaptable, constantly being shaped by our experiences.

Learning: The Brain's Rehearsal

Think of learning a new skill, like playing the piano or riding a bike. At first, it's challenging, but with practice, it becomes easier. This is neuroplasticity in action. When we learn something new, our brain forms new connections and strengthens them with practice, much like a musician rehearsing a new piece until it's flawless.

Memory: The Orchestra's Archive

Our memories are like the orchestra's sheet music, stored and retrieved when needed. Neuroplasticity plays a key role in how memories are formed and retrieved. Every time we recall a memory, our brain slightly rewrites it, potentially changing the details, much like tweaking a music score.

Recovery: The Comeback Concert

One of the most inspiring aspects of neuroplasticity is its role in recovery from injury. When part of the brain is damaged, like in a stroke, other parts can learn to take over the lost functions, akin to a violinist filling in for an absent cellist. This ability is crucial in rehabilitation therapies for stroke patients or those with brain injuries.

The Darker Notes: Over-Adaptation

Just as neuroplasticity can have positive effects, it can also lead to negative changes. For instance, in chronic pain, the brain might become overly sensitive, like an orchestra that plays too loudly. Understanding this aspect can help in developing treatments for such conditions.

Implications for Everyday Life

The concept of neuroplasticity is empowering. It suggests that our brains are not fixed but are continually evolving. It means that with the right practice and experiences, we can train our brains to think, feel, and perceive in new ways, enhancing our abilities and wellbeing.

In Conclusion

Neuroplasticity, the brain's ability to adapt and rewire itself, is a testament to the incredible potential and resilience of the human mind. Just like a versatile orchestra, our brain can adapt to new challenges and recover from setbacks, constantly evolving with every new experience. This knowledge not only gives us hope for recovery and growth but also inspires us to keep learning and exploring the limitless possibilities of our minds.

Chapter 4: Sensory Echoes

Imagine you are in a world where each sensation tells a unique story. This is the realm of our senses, a place where simple signals are transformed into the rich experiences that make up our daily lives. In "Sensory Echoes," we'll explore this fascinating process in an easy and engaging way.

The Concert of the Senses

Our brain is like a concert hall, with each sense playing its own instrument. These senses - sight, hearing, smell, taste, and touch - work together to create the symphony of our perceptions.

Sight: The World in Color

Sight is like the lead violin in an orchestra, capturing the world in vivid color and motion. Light enters our eyes and is converted into signals, much like a camera capturing a scene. These signals are sent to the brain, which interprets them as the images we see. It's a complex process, but at its core, it's about turning light into the visual world around us.

Hearing: The Symphony of Sound

Hearing is akin to the piano, translating vibrations into the rich tapestry of sounds. These vibrations, or sound waves, are captured by our ears and converted into signals. Our brain then interprets these signals as different sounds, whether it's the melody of a song or the voice of a loved one.

Smell and Taste: The Flavorful Duo

Smell and taste are like the woodwinds and brass in an orchestra, often working together to create the experience of flavor. Smell captures the scents in the air, while taste detects the flavors in our food. These sensations are combined in our brain to give us the delicious tastes we enjoy.

Touch: The Tactile Dance

Touch is like the percussion section, providing rhythm and depth to our sensory experience. Our skin is sensitive to pressure, temperature, and texture. These sensations are transmitted to the brain, allowing us to feel the warmth of a hug or the texture of a fabric.

The Brain's Role: The Conductor

Just as a conductor guides an orchestra, our brain integrates these sensory signals into a cohesive experience. It prioritizes some sensations over others, like focusing on a friend's voice in a noisy room. This integration allows us to interact with and understand our environment in a seamless way.

Learning from Sensory Echoes

By understanding how our senses work, we gain insights into our interaction with the world. It helps us appreciate the complexities of experience - how a particular smell can evoke a memory or how the texture of an object can tell us about its properties.

Chapter 5: Memory's Vault

Welcome to the fascinating world of memory, a place where our past experiences, knowledge, and emotions are stored. It's like a vast, intricate vault where each memory is a precious treasure. In "Memory's Vault," we will unravel the mysteries of memory in a simple and engaging way, exploring how it shapes our identity and our understanding of the world.

The Tapestry of Memory

Imagine memory as a tapestry, woven from countless threads of experiences, facts, and emotions. Each thread represents a different type of memory, contributing to the overall picture of our past.

Short-Term Memory: The Sketchpad

Short-term memory is like a sketchpad. It holds information temporarily, like a phone number you just heard. This memory is fleeting, often lasting only a few seconds to a minute unless we actively focus on it or repeat it to ourselves.

Long-Term Memory: The Deep Archive

Long-term memory is the deep, vast archive where our experiences, knowledge, and skills are stored for long periods. This type of memory includes everything from your childhood memories to how to ride a bike. It's more permanent and can last a lifetime.

Explicit Memory: The Storyteller

Explicit memory, or declarative memory, is like a storyteller. It includes the memories we can consciously recall and describe, like the details of a birthday party or the capital of a country.

Implicit Memory: The Silent Performer

Implicit memory works silently in the background. It includes the skills and habits we've learned but don't consciously think about, like tying shoelaces or riding a bicycle. This type of memory is automatic and often goes unnoticed.

How Memories are Formed and Stored

Creating a memory is like painting a picture. When we experience something, our brain processes and encodes the information. It's like sketching the outlines and filling in the colors. The more we focus on or revisit this memory, the stronger and more detailed it becomes.

Memories are stored across different areas of the brain. The hippocampus, a seahorse-shaped area deep in the brain, acts like a key librarian, helping to form and retrieve explicit memories. Other areas, like the amygdala for emotions and the cerebellum for motor skills, also play crucial roles.

Forgetting: The Art of Letting Go

Forgetting is not a failure of the brain but a natural and important process. It's like cleaning up the tapestry, removing the threads that are no longer needed to make room for new ones. Forgetting helps us prioritize important information and learn from new experiences.

In Conclusion

Our memories shape our identity, our decisions, and our interactions with the world. Understanding memory is like having a map of this vast vault, helping us appreciate the richness of our past and the potential of our future. As we close this chapter, remember that each memory, whether vivid or faded, is a vital part of the beautiful tapestry that is your life.

Chapter 6: The Emotional Tide

Embark on a journey to the heart of our emotions, where feelings like joy, sadness, anger, and love are not just fleeting moments, but powerful tides that shape our lives. In this chapter we will explore the fascinating world of emotions and how they are intricately woven into the fabric of our brains.

Emotions: The Colors of Life

Imagine emotions as colors, each adding a unique shade to our experiences. Emotions are not just reactions to the world around us; they are essential guides that help us navigate through life. They tell us what to approach or avoid, connect us with others, and are crucial for our survival.

The Brain's Emotional Landscape

The Amygdala: The Alarm System

The amygdala, deep in the brain, acts like an alarm system. It quickly evaluates situations for potential danger or reward and triggers emotional responses. When you feel fear seeing a snake, it's your amygdala in action.

The Prefrontal Cortex: The Emotional Manager

The prefrontal cortex, located at the front of the brain, is like the manager of emotions. It helps us understand and regulate our feelings, deciding how to react. It's the part that calms you down after the initial scare from the snake.

The Hippocampus: The Memory Link

The hippocampus, involved in memory, links emotions to past experiences. It's why certain smells or sounds can evoke strong emotional memories, like the comfort of a childhood dish or the excitement of a favorite song.

The Evolution of Emotions

Emotions have evolved as a survival mechanism. Fear makes us flee from danger, while love and social bonding ensure the care of offspring and the survival of the group. Even complex emotions like guilt or pride have evolved to help us live and work better in social communities.

The Flow of Emotions

Processing emotions is like the ebb and flow of a tide. When we experience an emotion, a wave of neurological and chemical changes sweeps through our brain, affecting our thoughts, feelings, and even physical state. It's a complex dance between different brain regions, neurotransmitters, and our body's responses.

Emotions and Wellbeing

Understanding our emotional brain is key to our wellbeing. It helps us manage stress, build better relationships, and navigate the ups and downs of life. Emotions are not just reactions; they are a language our brain uses to communicate with us.

In Conclusion

By understanding how they are processed in the brain, we gain insight into why we feel the way we do and how we can harness these feelings for a richer, more fulfilling life. Emotions are the music of our internal world, playing a symphony that resonates with the story of being human.

Chapter 7: Shadowed Minds

In this chapter, we delve into the world of neuropsychological disorders, a realm where the brain's usual harmony faces challenges. This chapter will explore these disorders in an approachable way, shedding light on their symptoms and what they reveal about the everyday workings of the brain.

Understanding Neuropsychological Disorders

Neuropsychological disorders are like disruptions in the brain's usual symphony. They can affect how we think, feel, and behave, often making everyday tasks challenging. By studying these disorders, we gain invaluable insights into the normal functioning of the brain.

Memory Disorders: Lost Threads

Imagine your memory as a tapestry of experiences. Memory disorders, like Alzheimer's disease, fray this tapestry. People with these conditions may forget familiar faces, recent events, or even basic tasks. Observing these symptoms helps us understand how memory is woven into our brain's fabric.

Mood Disorders: Unbalanced Harmonies

Mood disorders, including depression and bipolar disorder, are like an unbalanced musical scale, where the brain's emotional regulation is disrupted. These conditions can lead to prolonged sadness, extreme highs and lows, and a loss of interest in activities. They reveal the delicate balance required for emotional stability.

Anxiety Disorders: Amplified Alarms

Anxiety disorders can be likened to an over-sensitive alarm system in the brain. They often involve excessive worry, fear, or panic, even in safe situations. Studying these disorders illuminates how the brain processes fear and stress.

Behavioral Disorders: Disrupted Rhythms

Disorders like ADHD (Attention Deficit Hyperactivity Disorder) disrupt the brain's natural rhythms, affecting attention, impulsivity, and activity levels. They show us how the brain organizes thoughts and actions, maintaining focus and self-control.

The Brain's Resilience and Adaptability

These disorders highlight the brain's incredible resilience and adaptability. Treatments and therapies, like medication, counseling, or behavioral strategies, can help re-tune the brain's functions, much like fine-tuning a musical instrument.

A Compassionate Perspective

Studying neuropsychological disorders also teaches us compassion and understanding. It reminds us that everyone's brain plays a different tune and that those with these conditions experience the world in unique ways.

In Conclusion

This chapter is not just about the challenges of these conditions but also about hope, understanding, and the endless potential for learning and adaptation.

Chapter 8: The Conscious Conundrum

In this chapter, we embark on a journey to unravel one of the most intriguing mysteries of the human mind: consciousness. This chapter will explore what consciousness means from a neuropsychological perspective, discussing various theories and debates in a manner that is accessible and engaging for everyone.

Defining Consciousness: The Enigma

Consciousness is like the light that illuminates our inner and outer worlds. It's our awareness of ourselves and our environment. Despite its familiarity, consciousness remains one of the most elusive and debated topics in neuropsychology. It's like trying to describe the flavor of water – something so integral and omnipresent yet challenging to define.

Theories of Consciousness: Different Lenses

The Theater of the Mind

One theory compares consciousness to a stage in a theater, with different thoughts and perceptions coming into the spotlight of our attention. This theory suggests that our brain selectively focuses on certain experiences while filtering out others, similar to how a spotlight highlights an actor on stage.

The Integrated Information Theory

Imagine a network of interconnected lights, each one influencing the other. This theory proposes that consciousness arises from the ability of the brain to integrate and process information in a complex way. The more interconnected and integrated these neural processes are, the more conscious the experience.

The Global Workspace Theory

This theory likens consciousness to a bustling office space, where information is shared and broadcasted across different departments (or brain regions). Consciousness emerges when information is distributed across this global workspace, becoming accessible to various cognitive processes.

Debates in Consciousness: Unanswered Questions

The study of consciousness is full of ongoing debates and questions. What is its purpose? Is it a byproduct of complex neural processes, or does it play a more active role in our survival? How do we measure it, and can other creatures be conscious in the way humans are?

Consciousness in Everyday Life

Understanding consciousness enhances our appreciation of everyday experiences. It makes us wonder about the nature of our thoughts, dreams, and perceptions. It also raises ethical considerations, such as how we define and respect consciousness in others, including in non-human animals and potentially in artificial intelligences in the future.

In Conclusion

This journey into consciousness is not just a scientific exploration, but a personal and philosophical adventure into the heart of what it means to be aware and alive.

Chapter 9: The Altered States

In this chapter, we step into the fascinating world where external influences, from substances to practices like meditation, can change the way our brain functions and how we behave. This chapter will navigate through these intriguing changes in a simple, engaging, and accessible way.

Substances and the Brain: A Delicate Balance

The Impact of Drugs

Imagine your brain as a complex circuit board. Drugs, whether they are caffeine from your morning coffee or prescription medications, interact with this circuitry. Some substances, like alcohol, can slow down the signals in the brain, like dimming the lights in a room. Others, like caffeine, can make these signals faster, brightening the room. This change in brain activity can alter how we think, feel, and act.

The Healing Power of Medications

Medications prescribed by doctors aim to restore the balance in the brain's circuitry, much like fixing a flickering light. For example, antidepressants help adjust the levels of certain chemicals in the brain to alleviate symptoms of depression.

Meditation and Mindfulness: The Calming Effect

The Practice of Meditation

Meditation is like a quiet symphony in the mind. It often involves focusing attention and cultivating a state of calm. Regular meditation can change how certain areas of the brain communicate, much like how a conductor guides an orchestra to play in harmony. This can lead to improved focus, reduced stress, and a sense of wellbeing.

Mindfulness in Daily Life

Mindfulness, a form of meditation, is about being fully present in the moment. It's like shining a spotlight on your current experience, noticing your thoughts, feelings, and environment without judgment. Practicing mindfulness can help reduce stress and improve emotional regulation.

External Influences: From Light to Sound

The Role of Light

Light, especially natural sunlight, can significantly impact our brain function and mood. It's like the sun that helps a garden grow. Exposure to natural light during the day can improve sleep, mood, and focus.

The Power of Sound

Sounds, from music to the noise in our environment, can also influence our brain function. Calming music can relax the brain, while constant loud noise can be disruptive, like a storm disturbing the garden.

In Conclusion

This chapter doesn't just explore these states; it offers a glimpse into how delicate and responsive our brain is to the external world. It reminds us that while some of these influences are within our control, like meditation or medication, others, like our environment, require us to adapt and find balance. Understanding these altered states equips us with knowledge to make informed choices about our brain health and wellbeing.

Chapter 10: Technological Mindscapes

In this chapter we journey through the remarkable ways modern technology is revolutionizing our understanding of the brain. From artificial intelligence (AI) to advanced imaging techniques, we'll explore these advancements in a way that's both easy to understand and captivating.

Artificial Intelligence: The Brain's Digital Reflection

AI and Brain Function

Think of AI as a mirror reflecting the complexities of the human brain. AI algorithms, inspired by the way our brain processes information, help researchers simulate and understand brain functions. For instance, by mimicking how neurons connect and communicate, AI can provide insights into learning and memory.

AI in Mental Health

AI is also emerging as a tool in mental health care. It can analyze patterns in speech or behavior that might be too subtle for humans to notice, potentially helping in the early detection of conditions like depression or anxiety.

Neuroimaging: A Window into the Brain

Seeing the Unseen

Neuroimaging technologies are like windows that let us peer into the brain's inner workings. Techniques like MRI (Magnetic Resonance Imaging) and PET (Positron Emission Tomography) scans provide detailed images of the brain's structure and activity. This is akin to mapping a vast city, revealing the intricate networks that underlie our thoughts, feelings, and behaviors.

Understanding Brain Disorders

These imaging technologies are particularly valuable in understanding and diagnosing brain disorders. They can show changes in the brain's structure in conditions like Alzheimer's disease or monitor brain activity in disorders like epilepsy.

Virtual Reality: A New Frontier for Therapy

Immersive Experiences

Virtual reality (VR) creates immersive digital environments that can be used for therapeutic purposes. For instance, VR can simulate environments to help treat conditions like PTSD (Post-Traumatic Stress Disorder) or phobias by gradually exposing patients to their triggers in a controlled, safe setting.

Enhancing Rehabilitation

VR technology is also being used in neurological rehabilitation. It can create interactive, engaging scenarios for patients recovering from strokes or brain injuries, aiding in their recovery by improving motivation and engagement.

Wearable Technology: Monitoring the Brain in Daily Life

Everyday Brain Health

Wearable technology, like smartwatches and fitness trackers, is beginning to include features that monitor aspects of brain health, such as stress levels or sleep quality. This continuous monitoring can provide valuable data for understanding how our daily lives affect our brain function.

In Conclusion

This chapter is not just a chapter about the brain and technology; it's a glimpse into the future of neuropsychology. As we continue to integrate these advanced technologies into our study of the brain, we open new doors to understanding ourselves and enhancing our mental health. This chapter invites readers to marvel at the possibilities and to appreciate how technology is helping us map the most complex and fascinating terrain known to mankind – the human brain.

Chapter 11: The Neuroethical Dilemma

In this chapter, we venture into the realm of ethics in neuropsychology. This chapter navigates the complex ethical questions that arise as we delve deeper into the brain's mysteries and capabilities, from enhancing brain functions to protecting brain privacy. We'll explore these topics in a straightforward and engaging manner, making them accessible to all.

Neuroenhancement: The Quest for Supercharged Brains

Cognitive Enhancers

Imagine a pill that could make your brain work faster or better. This is the concept of neuroenhancement, using drugs or other means to improve cognitive functions like memory or attention. While this sounds like a superpower, it raises ethical questions. Is it fair for some people to have access to these enhancers while others don't? Could this create a society of 'haves' and 'have-nots' based on who can afford or access these enhancements?

The Ethics of Brain Enhancement

Beyond fairness, there's the question of safety and long-term effects. Are we comfortable altering our brain's chemistry, and what are the risks involved? Neuroenhancement challenges us to consider the balance between the pursuit of improved abilities and the potential consequences.

Brain Privacy: A New Frontier

Neuroimaging and Privacy

Advanced neuroimaging can potentially reveal our thoughts, feelings, and even intentions. This raises the question of brain privacy. How do we ensure that this deeply personal information is protected? Who should have access to it, and under what circumstances?

The Right to Cognitive Liberty

Cognitive liberty is the right to control our own mental processes. As neurotechnology advances, ensuring this right becomes increasingly important. It's about protecting the privacy of our inner thoughts and ensuring that individuals are not coerced into using neurotechnology.

The Ethics of Neuropsychological Research

Informed Consent

In neuropsychological research, informed consent is crucial. Participants must be fully aware of what the research entails, including any risks or benefits. This is especially important in studies that involve vulnerable populations or potentially risky procedures.

Balancing Risk and Benefit

Researchers must balance the potential benefits of their work with the risks to participants. This includes considering the long-term impacts of their research on individuals and society.

Neurotechnology in the Legal System

Brain-Based Evidence

The use of neurotechnology in the legal system, like using brain scans as evidence in court, raises ethical questions. How accurate and reliable are these methods? Could they lead to privacy invasions or unfair judgments?

In Conclusion

This chapter opens a dialogue on the ethical considerations in neuropsychology. It's not just about the amazing capabilities of modern neuroscience but also about the responsibility that comes with these advancements. As we continue to explore the brain's potential, we must also consider the ethical implications, ensuring that our journey into the mind respects our values and rights as individuals. This chapter is an invitation to ponder these critical questions, guiding us towards a future where neuropsychological advancements are made with care, responsibility, and ethical integrity.

Epilogue: Beyond the Gray Horizon

As we reach the conclusion of our journey through the fascinating world of neuropsychology , we pause to reflect on the future of this ever-evolving field. This epilogue will explore the boundless potential for discoveries, the lingering questions, and the exciting possibilities that lie ahead in neuropsychology, all presented in a way that's both engaging and easy to understand.

The Uncharted Territories of the Brain

The Mystery of Consciousness

One of the greatest mysteries that continues to captivate neuropsychologists is the nature of consciousness. How does a collection of neurons and chemical signals create the rich tapestry of human experience? The pursuit of this question promises not only scientific advancement but also deeper philosophical understanding of what it means to be human.

Unlocking the Secrets of Memory

Memory remains a largely uncharted territory. We are just beginning to understand how memories are formed, stored, and why they fade. Future research could unlock the secrets to enhancing memory, treating memory disorders, and even understanding how our memories shape our identity.

The Promise of Technology

Neurotechnology and Brain Health

Advancements in technology hold immense promise for neuropsychology. Imagine devices that can not only read brain activity more accurately but also intervene to treat disorders. This could revolutionize the treatment of conditions like depression, epilepsy, and even traumatic brain injuries.

Artificial Intelligence and Brain Research

AI is set to transform neuropsychological research. It could help in modeling brain processes, predicting neurological disorders, and even in developing personalized treatment plans based on individual brain patterns.

The Ethical Frontier

Navigating the Ethical Landscape

With great power comes great responsibility. As we step into the future, the ethical implications of neuropsychological research and its applications will become even more significant. Issues of cognitive liberty, privacy, and the implications of brain-enhancing technologies will require thoughtful consideration and public discourse.

A Future of Collaboration

Interdisciplinary Approaches

The future of neuropsychology lies in collaboration across disciplines. By combining insights from psychology, neuroscience, medicine, technology, and even philosophy, we can create a more holistic understanding of the brain and the mind.

In Conclusion

The journey of neuropsychology is far from complete; it continues to stand at the frontier of science, beckoning us to explore the vast and unknown territories of the human mind. This epilogue serves as a reminder that the pursuit of knowledge is an endless adventure, and the mysteries of the brain offer one of the most exciting frontiers yet to be fully explored.

About Freudian Trips

Welcome to Freudian Trips, your dedicated platform for diving deep into the world of psychology. We are more than just a YouTube channel or a book publisher. We are a beacon of enlightenment, making complex psychological concepts accessible and engaging for all.

Our YouTube channel is a rich repository of psychology made simple. We take the profound and often complex ideas from the world of psychology and break them down into digestible, easy-to-understand content. From the foundational theories of Freud to the cognitive insights of Piaget, we cover a broad spectrum of psychological schools and thoughts, making psychology accessible to everyone, regardless of their background or prior knowledge.

As a book publisher, we take the same approach, transforming intricate psychological theories into comprehensible narratives. Our books are not just collections of words, but vessels of wisdom that make psychology approachable and relatable. We believe that psychology should not be confined to academic circles, but should be available to all who seek to understand the human mind and behavior.

At Freudian Trips, we believe in the power of curiosity and the pursuit of knowledge. We are here to stoke the fires of your curiosity, to guide you on your intellectual journey, and to help you navigate the fascinating world of psychology.

If you are someone who is not afraid to question, to explore, and to learn, then you are in the right place. Join us on this journey of exploration, as we make psychology easy to understand, one concept at a time.

Be sure to visit our Youtube channel at: www.freudiantrips.com/youtube

You can also visit us on the web at www.freudiantrips.com

Welcome to The Freudian Trip community. Stay curious. Stay enlightened.

* 9 7 9 8 8 6 7 3 7 3 4 9 8 *